AIR TRAFFIC CONTROLLER

COOL VOCATIONAL CAREERS

Published in the United States of America by Cherry Lake Publishing
Ann Arbor, Michigan
www.cherrylakepublishing.com

Content Adviser: Kate Hale, FAA, Air Traffic Division/New England (retired)
Reading Adviser: Marla Conn MS, Ed., Literacy specialist, Read-Ability, Inc.

Photo Credits: © Angelo Giampiccolo/Shutterstock, cover, 1; © iurii/Shutterstock, 5; © Stockbyte/Thinkstock, 6;
© Daily Mail/Rex / Alamy Stock Photo, 7; © HultonArchive/istock, 10; © Getty Images News/Thinkstock, 13, 16, 27;
© Gary718 | Dreamstime.com - Ground Crew Guides A Jet To The Gate Photo, 14; © marlee/Shutterstock, 18;
© Burben/Shutterstock, 21; © Phfw22 | Dreamstime.com - Busy Airport Photo, 22; © Steve Debenport/istock, 24;
© Sergey Furtaev/Shutterstock, 28

Library of Congress Cataloging-in-Publication Data
CIP data has been filed and is available at catalog.loc.gov.

Cherry Lake Publishing would like to acknowledge the work of the Partnership for 21st Century Learning.
Please visit www.p21.org for more information.

Printed in the United States of America
Corporate Graphics

ABOUT THE AUTHOR

Ellen Labrecque is a freelance writer living in Yardley, Pennsylvania. Previously, she was a senior editor at *Sports Illustrated Kids*. Ellen loves to travel and then learn about new places and people she can write about in her books.

TABLE OF CONTENTS

CHAPTER 1

One Hundred Years and Counting

Sam pressed his nose against the plane window. He saw white fluffy clouds against a bright blue sky. Sam was on vacation with his family. They were flying across the United States—from New York to California!

"It's like we have the sky all to ourselves!" Sam exclaimed to his dad, sitting next to him.

"Not *exactly*, son," his dad said with a laugh. "There are around 7,000 other airplanes flying over the United States right this moment!"

"No way!" Sam said. "So why isn't there a big traffic jam in the sky? How do all these flying planes know where the other ones are?"

"That's the job of **air traffic control specialists**," his dad said. "They keep planes from crashing into each other. Let me explain."

Airplanes are a popular and efficient way to travel.

An air traffic control specialist's job is to organize airplanes so that they move safely at all times, both in the air and on the ground. Controllers provide instructions and information to pilots. The pilot in command of an airplane is responsible for making the decisions about the plane's operation. Pilots use the information and instructions provided by air traffic controllers to take off, fly, and land safely. Every year, more than three billion passengers are carried safely through the skies. Sam's flight is one of more than 100,000 flights made each day by **commercial airliners**,

Air travel began in the early twentieth century.

private airplanes, and military aircraft traveling these invisible highways.

The air traffic control system is a huge spiderweb of people, equipment, and services. This system supports safe and **efficient** flights all over the world. For flights to be safe and efficient, everyone must be able to work together. The United States air traffic system is the safest in the world!

The first commercial flight with a paying passenger on board took off more than 100 years ago, on January 1, 1914. The flight took 23 minutes and flew across the bay from St. Petersburg to

Tampa, Florida. There were no controllers in the United States then. And there were still none when airplanes began carrying the mail in 1920. There were no **navigation aids** along the routes. Airmail pilots often got lost and could not fly at night. Concerned citizens built bonfires at landing fields near towns. These bonfires were the first step toward today's modern system of **airways**.

21st Century Content

The National Aeronautics and Space Administration (NASA) has teamed up with the **Federal Aviation Administration** (FAA) for an online educational project for kids called Smart Skies. The project teaches kids the skills needed to be an air traffic controller using real-life math and science problems. You can check out the project's math games at http://smartskies.nasa.gov.

"Being an air traffic controller is like playing the ultimate video game," says one Smart Skies teacher. "But you have to be right every time."

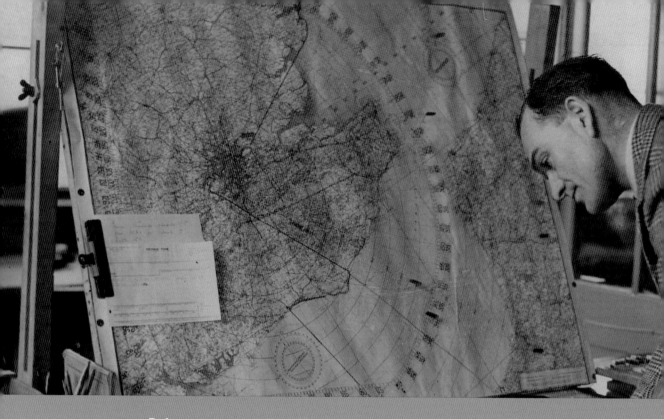

Before computers, air traffic controllers relied on paper maps.

Lighted **beacons** replaced the bonfires. These were lamps on
top of towers 51 feet (15.5 meters) high. By 1923, there were 289
beacon towers between Chicago, Illinois, and Cheyenne,
Wyoming. The towers' lights rotated every 10 seconds, making
them appear to be flashing. These lights made it possible for
airplanes to carry mail across the country at night. The beacons
were used to mark airport locations and routes for airplanes
to follow.

Beacons using radio beams to guide pilots replaced the light
beacons. In 1930, the first **air traffic control tower** was

established in Cleveland, Ohio. Two-way radio made it possible for controllers on the ground to talk with pilots in the air. This was a great improvement from the days when people on the ground could only communicate with pilots by waving flags!

World War II (1939–1945) brought incredible new **technology** that allowed airplanes to fly higher, faster, and farther. Women began working as air traffic controllers for the first time. The war also brought the discovery of radar, or radio detection and ranging. A radar transmitter sends out invisible radio waves. When the radio waves hit a solid object,

21st Century Content

A large variety of planes was used in World War II. Trainer aircraft helped pilots and airmen learn the difficult skill of flying. Cargo aircraft carried supplies across Europe. Attack aircraft dropped bombs. Several countries also used seaplanes, which are capable of taking off from and landing on water!

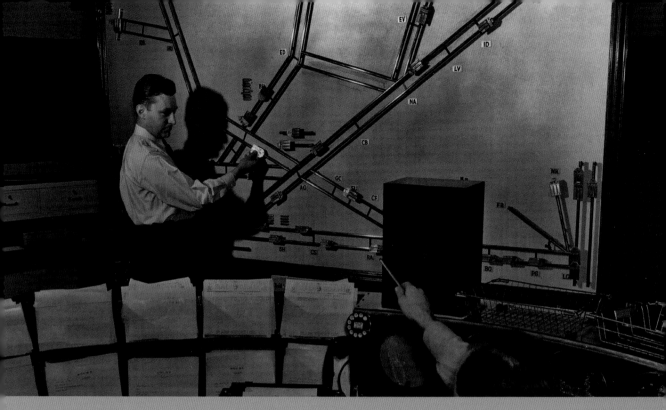

These air traffic controllers are using models of planes to track the real planes' movement.

they bounce back. A radar receiver receives the waves as they bounce back. A screen displays the object against which the radio waves bounced. Radar can be used to identify the location, altitude, direction of movement, and speed of moving objects such as airplanes.

The International Civil **Aviation** Organization (ICAO), a special agency of the United Nations, was formed in 1947. Members of the ICAO come from 190 countries. They agree on the air traffic rules that their countries follow for safe, secure air travel.

In 1952, passengers began flying on aircraft with jet engines. The jet age had begun! Jet engines allowed larger airplanes to fly longer distances. By 1958, more people were traveling across the Atlantic Ocean in airplanes than on ships. More airplanes carrying more passengers increased the need for more air traffic control workers around the world.

The Federal Aviation Administration (FAA) was created this same year. It is a large governing body in charge of the entire air traffic control system in the United States. It handles more than 100,000 flights a day. The number is expected to grow to 125,000 by 2035!

Computers brought the age of automation to air traffic control. Computers, **simulators**, and satellite technology are bringing challenges and change to air traffic control. One thing that has not changed is the need for air traffic control specialists. They will continue to help ensure the safe, efficient, and orderly flow of airplanes through the sky.

CHAPTER 2

A Giant Orchestra

Air traffic control is like a giant orchestra. When each controller does his or her job, airplanes fly safely across the sky, making sweet music.

The Air Traffic Control System Command Center in Warrenton, Virginia, is like the conductor of the orchestra. It sets the traffic flow over the entire United States each and every day. It plans ways to prevent **congestion** problems before they even happen. Weather is one thing that the controllers have to consider, since rain, snow, or fog might delay flights.

The command center has 22 Air Route Traffic Control Centers spread across the country. Each center is in charge of a certain amount of geographic airspace. A typical center is usually in

The control tower at every airport must be monitored around the clock every day.

charge of 100,000 square miles (259,000 square kilometers).

Melissa Holmes has spent 12 years as an air traffic manager at one of the control centers in Fremont, California. She works 40 hours a week and oversees all the air traffic operations at the center. She provides information to other controllers about equipment or weather problems. She also trains many new controllers.

All the control centers operate 24 hours a day, 7 days a week. The controllers work rotating shifts, including nights, weekends, and holidays.

The ground crew helps planes take off and land.

Let's meet some of the other members of the air traffic control "orchestra."

The tower controller works at an airport and manages all the aircraft taking off from and landing there.

In the tower, *the ground controller* is responsible for ground traffic at the airport, the aircraft, and vehicles. The ground controller notifies the pilot when it is safe for the aircraft to be pushed away from the gate/terminal and gives directions to the pilot to taxi or move toward the active runway. The airplane joins the other planes in line for takeoff. Ground controllers also give

21st Century Content

If air traffic controllers don't communicate clearly, the results can be deadly. A 1977 crash at an airport in Spain, where nearly 600 people were killed, happened partly because the controllers and pilots used words and phrases that weren't part of the standard set of commands.

This approach controller watches for planes coming into and leaving the airport.

directions to airplanes after they land and guide them back to the gate/terminal.

The local controller in the tower advises the pilot when it is safe for the airplane to enter the runway. This controller keeps departing and landing aircraft a safe distance from each other. The local controller clears aircraft for takeoff and gives clearances to land. Shortly after the airplane is in the air, the local controller transfers control to the departure controller, who is located at the approach control facility.

The approach controller works in a dark radar room.

Sometimes these rooms are located at an airport, but often they are located many miles away. These controllers work different positions or sectors within the approach control room. The departure controller organizes all the airborne airplanes leaving the airport area and the arrival controller lines up the airplanes approaching or heading toward the airport. When an airplane has climbed to a certain altitude, the approach controller transfers responsibility to the en route controller.

The en route controller is sometimes called a center controller. This person works at large Air Route Traffic Control Centers, along with hundreds of other controllers. En route controllers separate

Life and Career Skills

Working in air traffic control is one of the most stressful jobs a person can have. Why is this the case? People's lives are your responsibility as they fly across the sky! What are ways to reduce stress working as an air traffic controller? Would exercising regularly be helpful? How about getting enough sleep every night? What are other ways that an air traffic controller could reduce stress levels?

Throughout an entire flight, many different controllers pay attention to the same plane.

airplanes at higher altitudes. They provide information and directions for a flight once it has climbed. Each en route controller works in a different zone, or area, and they transfer responsibility to each other, as the airplane travels en route, or across the sky. When the airplane reaches a different center's airspace, the controller transfers responsibility to that new center.

This **relay** continues along the airplane's route until it is closer to its destination airport. The en route controller instructs the pilot to descend to a lower altitude, then transfers responsibility to an approach controller, who will line the airplane up with the runway being used and hand the airplane off to the tower controller for landing. After landing, the ground controller takes over. The relay is complete when the airplane reaches the arrival gate at the terminal.

CHAPTER 3

In Demand

Controller, Boeing Tower: "Piper 7787 Foxtrot cleared for takeoff, runway one three right, fly MERCER departure."

Pilot: "Piper 7787 Foxtrot cleared for takeoff, rolling."

This is what you might hear if you were listening to the conversation between an air traffic controller and the pilot of a private airplane. Air traffic controllers provide services to pilots no matter how big or small their airplanes may be.

The FAA expects to hire 6,300 new air traffic controllers from now until 2020. Many of these new hires will have learned air traffic control skills in the military. However, air traffic controller jobs do not require a college degree. If you have worked for three years at any job, you can apply. You do not have to be a pilot or know how to talk in aviation code like the Boeing tower

Air traffic controllers need excellent eyesight and the ability to focus mentally.

controller and the pilot. You do need to be between 18 and 30 years old and pass medical and drug screening tests. You also need to have at least 20/20 vision in each eye separately, either with or without glasses.

You also have to pass two other tests. One is a security clearance exam, which makes sure you're a good U.S. citizen. The other is a pre-application test. This test will show how well you can read, write, and speak English. It will also determine if you can think and work quickly to solve many different kinds of problems. Good reading, math, and science skills are

Because so much is at stake, FAA training is very rigorous.

important. The test is taken on a computer and takes about 8 hours to complete.

If you are hired, you will attend a training program at the FAA Academy in Oklahoma City. The program lasts between 7 and 15 weeks, depending on the type of controller you are training to be. Here are some of the things you will learn.

- Aviation terms and codes
- FAA rules and guidelines
- Weather conditions as they apply to flights
- How to use computers and radar equipment
- Skills for being a good team member

21st Century Content

The world's busiest airport is the Hartsfield-Jackson Atlanta International Airport. It serves 250,000 passengers a day, with more than 2,500 arriving and departing planes. Leaving from this airport, passengers can reach more than 225 destinations in 51 countries!

"You have to be on your A-game all the time to be an air traffic controller at this busy of an airport," says FAA manager Melissa Holmes.

Future air traffic controllers may need to pass some difficult math tests.

While you are at the academy, you will be given "pass or fail" tests. For example, you might be asked to use a pencil and paper to draw from memory all the airways in a certain area of airspace. Or you may be asked to quickly solve problems without the help of a computer or calculator. If you do not pass these tests, you will not be allowed to continue attending the academy.

After graduation from the academy, you may spend two to four years completing extra training. This may be done on the job and in classrooms. Working with experienced controllers is the best way to prepare for the responsibilities of a fully qualified controller.

Air traffic controllers in the United States earn good salaries for their hard work. Beginning controllers earn about $45,000 per year. Experienced controllers can sometimes earn more than $160,000. A number of things, such as location and years of experience, determine exact salaries. For example, an experienced controller working at a major airport may earn more money than a beginning controller working at an airport with fewer flights. Air traffic controllers must retire when they are 56 years old, except in very rare cases.

CHAPTER 4

Into the Future

Do you like using computers and cell phones to help you with directions and maps? If so, you might enjoy working as an air traffic controller—especially at this time in history!

Work on the Next Generation Air Transportation System began in 2007 and plans to be complete by 2030. This $32 billion project, known as NextGen, uses the latest technology to meet increasing air traffic control demands. The plan is designed by the FAA to improve safety as more people and cargo travel through the airways.

NextGen technology moves away from ground-based radar to satellite navigation. The FAA believes this change will reduce flight time, save fuel, and reduce noise. Much of this technology will make air traffic control systems more accurate.

Air traffic control technology is constantly improving.

For example, the En Route Automation Modernization system lets controllers track 1,900 aircraft at the same time. This number is up from 1,100 a couple of years ago. The system's satellite-based technology updates data every second. This is much faster than radar, which updates every 4 to 12 seconds. Even in these few seconds, an aircraft can travel a great distance. This means airplanes can safely fly more direct routes and closer together. This will cut back on flight delays across the world.

Data Comm is another new program. It gives pilots information and services that used to be directed first to air

For as long as people fly planes, air traffic controllers are a necessity.

traffic controllers, who then gave it to the pilots. Delivering information to pilots directly saves on time and cuts back on delays.

What are the most important qualities future air traffic controllers should have? "They need to be able to make decisions quickly," says Melissa Holmes. "And most importantly, they need to have a long attention span. Paying close attention is key to the success of future air traffic controllers!"

Life and Career Skills

The National Air Traffic Controllers Association, or NATCA, is an organization that represents air traffic controllers all over the United States. But no matter where air traffic controllers are based, they all must be able to do specific things. They must speak clearly and calmly and listen carefully. They must work as a team member and follow rules completely. Making good decisions quickly and memorizing information easily are very important skills. Finally, controllers must write neatly and solve problems quickly.

How many of these skills do you have?

Think About It

Imagine if air traffic controllers didn't exist. Would airplanes be able to fly safely around the world? Can you think of other jobs that are needed to maintain the safety of people across the entire world?

NASA is hoping to someday soon send people to live on Mars. Maybe one day there will even be shuttles going back and forth between our planets. If this is the case, could air traffic controllers be used in outer space, too?

New high-definition cameras and radar are now allowing air traffic controllers to be hundreds of miles away from the airport where they are helping to land airplanes safely. Would you rather have air traffic controllers work from a tower nearby and see the airplanes they are landing? What are the pluses and minuses of this new type of technology?

For More Information

BOOKS

McMannamy, Jim. *My Daddy Is an Air Traffic Controller.* Essex, UK: JPM Publishing, 2013.

Whiteman, Philip. *Aircraft: The Definitive Visual History.* New York: DK Publishing, 2013.

WEB SITES

How Stuff Works—How Air Traffic Control Works
http://science.howstuffworks.com/transport/flight/modern/air-traffic-control.htm
Be sure to click through the flight image gallery!

Live Air Traffic—From Their Headsets to You
www.liveatc.net
Listen to real air traffic controllers doing their jobs.

National Air Traffic Controllers Association
www.natca.org
Under "resources" click on "Kids Corner" to see some activities and cool videos!

GLOSSARY

air traffic control specialists (AIR TRAF-ik kuhn-TROHL SPESH-uh-lists) people trained to keep aircraft safe and separated by providing information and services to pilots on the ground and in the air

air traffic control tower (AIR TRAF-ik kuhn-TROHL TOU-ur) a tall building at an airport, surrounded by glass windows at the top, where air traffic controllers work

airways (AIR-wayz) invisible flight paths (highways) in the sky

aviation (ay-vee-AY-shuhn) the practice and science of building and flying aircraft

beacons (BEE-kuhnz) lights or other signals used for guiding aircraft

commercial airliners (kuh-MUR-shuhl AIR-lye-nurz) planes that carry paying passengers at scheduled times

congestion (kuhn-JES-chun) so blocked up or full that it is difficult to move

efficient (i-FISH-uhnt) working very well and not wasting time or energy

Federal Aviation Administration (FED-ur-uhl ay-vee-AY-shuhn ad-min-uh-STRAY-shuhn) the United States agency responsible for the safe movement of aircraft

navigation aids (nav-uh-GAY-shuhn AYDZ) signals and markers used to guide airplanes

relay (REE-lay) passing along responsibilities much like a team race in which each member covers a portion of the total distance

simulators (SIM-yuh-lay-turz) models used for training and practice

technology (tek-NAH-luh-jee) the use of science and engineering to do practical things, such as making businesses more efficient

INDEX